Ashdon

The village of Ashdon, located three miles north-east of Saffron Waldon, lies on an ancient road within the picturesque rolling hills of the boulder clays of north-east Essex. It is surrounded by lush arable land and large areas of what was once a vast forest. Ashdon is mentioned in the Domesday Book but there was a settlement around the church for many centuries prior to this

Ashdon is steeped in history and has many interesting buildings. There were once 31 farms in the parish but today these have been amalgamated into nine much larger farmsteads and many of the old farmhouses in or close to the village have been converted into homes. All Saints Church (left) at the top of Church Hill off Walden Road was rebuilt in stone in the early 11th century; originally it was a wooden structure. The only remaining post mill, Bragg's Mill, situated at the end of Mill Lane, is currently being restored. Ashdon is host to a kite festival which is held at Waltons Park each year in early June. This old railway carriage (below) is the only trace of a small railway station that was once on the edge of the village; part of the branch rail link which ran between Bartlow and Audley End, the line was closed in May 1964. The Ashdon Village Collection, in Church Hill, is a museum of village life through the ages. Its fascinating displays cover agriculture, the home, fashion, shopping and entertainment.

Anmer

The tiny village of Anmer has an enviable location, situated midway between Sandringham and Houghton Hall in north Norfolk. It is a place where time seems to stand still – except, of course, when a keenly contested bowls match is taking place on the green beside the sports and social club

The main street in Anmer is lined with attractive flint and redbrick cottages, all with beautiful gardens. In the past, most of the inhabitants of the village worked on the Royal estate or at nearby Anmer Hall. The church of St Mary was built around the time when the great family of Calthorp were Lords of the Manor. Anmer passed from the Calthorps to the Coldham family in 1678, and memorials to the Coldhams can be seen inside the church, which is just visible through a huge canopy of mature broad-leaved trees. The parish now covers about 1,400 acres and is part of the Royal Estate at Sandringham; virtually all the houses in the village belong to the Sandringham Estate which also includes the local villages of Wolferton, West Newton, Appleton, Flitcham and Sherbourne.

ASHWELL

The picturesque village of Ashwell lies just west of the Icknield Way that links Letchworth to Royston in north-east Hertfordshire. Its name is derived from springs which are the source of the river Rhee, a main tributary of the Cam. The springs are situated under a copse of ash trees close to the eastern end of the high street

Archaeological evidence shows that people have lived in the Ashwell area since the stone age. The Ashwell Village Museum contains a vast array of fascinating artefacts including toys, tools, a man trap, even a black rat marking the time when the local area was ravaged by bubonic plague. The museum, housed in a 16th century town house, was opened in 1930 and also displays a number of items discovered in the village including a barbed flint arrow, Roman coins, glass and pottery as well as a copper coin of Cunobeline, a Celtic prince. During the 19th century brewing, digging for coprolite (fossilised human dung) and straw plaiting were the main industries in the village.

The 14th century church of St Mary the Virgin with its distinctive octagonal 176ft tower is seen here behind a set of pretty terraced cottages (above). The church is well known for its medieval drawings and writings, many of which have been cut into its soft internal walls. Some of the drawings depict images of old St Paul's cathedral and they also contain references to the plight of local survivors of the Black Death.

BARNHAM

Between Bury St Edmunds and Thetford, Barnham contains eleven thatched houses and a fine avenue of beech trees leading into the village from Euston Hall, the home of the Dukes of Grafton for over 300 years

In 1730 the second Duke of Grafton bought much of the land in and around the village; today, many of the village houses are still owned by the estate. Euston Hall, which is open to the public on certain days, has beautiful gardens and an unusual watermill designed to resemble a church. Its famous collection of paintings from the court of Charles II include works by the portrait painter Peter Lely, Van Dyck and George Stubbs, the greatest animal painter of the 18th century. Two hundred years ago Barnham was divided into two parishes – St Martin's and St Gregory's. All that remains today of St Martin's is its tower; the church of St Gregory still stands.

BIRCHAM

The restored windmill in Great Bircham, a few miles north-east of King's Lynn, is a great attraction for visitors. The village is set amidst gently rolling fertile farmland typical of this area of north Norfolk

At one time this part of East Anglia had over 300 mills grinding corn for cattle and for horse-feed and breadmaking. Today very few mill buildings remain and most of those are in ruins. Dating from 1846, Bircham has been restored and is the only mill in the area in working order and open to the public. Visitors can climb all five floors to the fan stage where there are panoramic views of the surrounding countryside.

The church of St Mary the Virgin, in the centre of the village, is well known for its peal of bells and one of its ancient bells is on display in the nave of the church On windy days, visitors to Bircham Mill (above) can see the sails and milling machinery in operation. The tea rooms and gallery, built on the site of the old granary, contain many historic tools and machinery linked to the ancient milling trade. Adjoining the mill is a bakery which still has its original coal-fired oven.

BLAKENEY

Between Wells-next-the-Sea and Sheringham on the north Norfolk coast, Blakeney is an enchanting and much-loved coastal village. In the past it was a very busy medieval commercial port. Today the once wide estuary has silted up and only smaller boats and pleasurecraft are able to weave their way through the marshes between the many sand hills and mud banks

Owned by the National Trust since 1912, Blakeney Point (below right), is a 3.5 mile sand and shingle spit, which can only be reached by boat or by walking along the beach from Cley. Boat trips can be booked from both Blakeney and Morston Quays. Blakeney Point is a world-renowned nature reserve and bird sanctuary where record numbers of birds and wild plants can be seen. The seal colony numbers around 400 and the common seals outnumber the grey seals. Migrating birds come here to feed and breed and it is not uncommon to see little, common, Sandwich and Arctic terns. Other regular visitors include oystercatchers, shelduck and ringed plover.

The village contains a large number of charming traditional flint cottages, many of which are used as holiday lets. The well-stocked village chandlery is a popular local amenity.

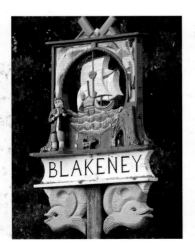

BLYTHBURGH

This captivating small village in Suffolk, a few miles west of Southwold, lies close to the banks of Blyth Water, a tidal lagoon. The village and its surrounding area have a fascinating history, rich in archaeological, literary, artistic and musical associations

The stunning medieval church of Holy Trinity (left and right) dominates the river estuary and is a much loved and useful beacon for travellers in the area. One of the grandest churches in Suffolk, it is known as the "Cathedral of the marshes" and is a regular venue for concerts during the summer Aldeburgh Festival. Suspended from the roof beams are 12 pairs of carved and painted angels (below). Some of the angels are peppered with lead shot. This probably came from the muskets of men in the 18th century who were paid by the churchwarden to shoot jackdaws in the church. At night Holy Trinity is floodlit, a familiar sight for travellers on the A12 from London to Yarmouth. Part of the Suffolk Heritage Coast, Blythburgh is surrounded by beautiful coastal walks through the surrounding woodlands and along the shore of Blyth Water.

THE BURNHAMS

Burnham Market is the largest of the wonderful cluster of villages known as the Burnhams. Situated just a stone's throw from the north Norfolk coast and close to Brancaster and Wells-next-the-Sea, it has remained unchanged for centuries. Its attractive main street centred on the wide village green is lined with a wide variety of independent specialist shops

Burnham Overy Staithe (above) is a honeypot for boating enthusiasts with its challenging tidal creek waters and traditional chandlery offering boat storage and repairs. Boat trips run from here to Scolt Head during the summer season.

A short distance inland to the south-east lies the smaller village of Burnham Thorpe. The great naval commander Admiral Horatio Nelson was born here in 1758 and learnt to sail in the creeks and inlets of the north Norfolk coast.

CASTLE ACRE

The picturesque and peaceful village of Castle Acre a few miles north of Swaffham is famous for the twin ruins of its castle and priory. This is one of the best examples of a planned Norman settlement anywhere in the country

After visiting the French monastery of Cluny William the Conqueror and his wife Gundrada were so impressed that they vowed to introduce the Cluniac order of monks to England. The priory they founded around 1090 at Castle Acre rapidly developed into one of the largest in the country. Today some of the priory lies in ruins (right) but much of the original building, including the prior's house and private chapel, still stand making it one of the best preserved monastic sites in England. The impressive castle was built by William de Warenne, first Earl of Surrey and a close supporter of William. Its remains (above) consist of huge earth banks surrounding a bailey; at one end stands a motte and the remains of a keep. The castle was used until the death of the last Warenne earl in 1347. The original and impressive stone bailey gatehouse which was used as an entrance to the castle stands in the centre of the village. Castle Acre contains a large number of flint and cobble cottages centred on Stocks Green (below), the attractive village green planted with large lime trees and once the site of the village stocks.

CASTLE HEDINGHAM

Situated just west of Halstead, Castle Hedingham is best known for its magnificent Norman keep. Built in 1140 by Aubrey de Vere, earl of Oxford, it is one of the best preserved castle keeps in Europe

Aubrey de Vere, one of William the Conqueror's main supporters, built Castle Hedingham on land granted to him by William for his support during the invasion of England. The keep (right) is the only medieval part of the castle to survive and today it forms a superb background for jousting tournaments (above) where history is brought to life with spectacular re-enactments featuring knights in armed combat, music, entertainment and dancing. The castle is surrounded by a beautiful old deer park with a 15th century Tudor bridge which replaced the castle drawbridge and spans the now dry moat leading to the inner bailey. The park has an unusual dovecote and attractive lake.

Castle Hedingham is home to the Colne Valley and Halstead Railway which was founded in 1974. It runs steam trains on a mile-long track along the Colne valley, once part of the original railway built in 1856 between Halstead and Haverhill. The twin village of Sible Hedingham lies to the south on the opposite bank of the river Colne.

CLARE

A beautiful small Suffolk market town situated between Melford and Haverhill on the north bank of the river Stour, Clare developed as a centre for the wool industry in the middle ages

This panoramic rooftop view of Clare (above) can be seen from the castle mound situated in Clare country park just two minutes walk from the town centre. The mound has remnants of the old stone castle keep and close by are the old railway track and station – the only railway line in the country ever to have been built inside castle grounds. The impressive roof and spire of the church of St Peter and St Paul is visible throughout the town, towering over the red-topped roofs of the houses clustered around. Many of the old houses in Clare are famous for their pargetting – a rough-cast decorative plasterwork applied to the outside walls, typical of many old buildings in this part of East Anglia. The Ancient House Museum on the High Street with its collection and database illustrating the history of the town is the start of the local town trail. This 15th century building has particularly fine pargetting on its front elevation.

CLAVERING

The pretty village of Clavering is located in rural north-west Essex approximately 10 miles from Stansted and 20 miles south of Cambridge. Many of the fascinating place names in the village such as "Cakebreads", "Chalkpit Lane" (also known as Gipsy Lane) and "Coffin Path" provide clues to Clavering's long and varied history

Traditional village signposts are a feature of villages in north Essex. Clavering's distinctive sign (below), designed by Carol Wilkinson, was erected in 1997. The design has a surround of clover and buttercups – both features of Clavering's heritage – with blacksmith's strapwork around its edges. The ford over the river Stort (below) is a picturesque feature of Clavering. Close to the water stands the thatched fordkeeper's cottage which claims to be the smallest house in Essex. In springtime the village is full of the wildflowers that grow along the streams and hedgerows. The name "Clavering" means "the place where clover grows". To the north of the parish church are the remains of the moated castle that once stood guard over the village.

CLEY NEXT THE SEA

In the Middle Ages Cley was a prosperous port on the Glaven estuary in north Norfolk, exporting large quantities of barley, oats, malt and wool. Today it is at the centre of an area of outstanding natural beauty and the Cley Marshes nature reserve is one of the best in the country

The size and scale of the heavily decorated church of St Margaret bears testament to the fact that this village was a vital port in late medieval England. Wealthy merchants, who had become prosperous as a result of trade with the Low Countries, built and re-built this church in its grand style over the centuries.

The picturesque 18th century Cley windmill (right) which stands close to the old quay on the north side of the village, is one of the best-loved landmarks on the north Norfolk coast. It has been restored and is now a guesthouse.

Cley Marshes is one of the country's premier nature reserves. Consisting of over 400 acres, this patchwork of freshwater pools, reed-beds, dykes, saline lagoons and grazing marshes has been managed by the Norfolk Naturalist Trust since 1926. It provides an ideal habitat for a wide variety of birds and birdwatching hides are situated around the site giving visitors good vantage points.

DEDHAM

The village of Dedham is set in glorious Dedham Vale, close to the river Stour which straddles the border of Suffolk and Essex. The Vale is known as "Constable Country" in memory of the famous landscape painter John Constable, a native of the area

Dedham prospered as a wool town in the Middle Ages and many of the fine buildings in the village date from this era, including the half-timbered Marlborough Head Hotel (above) in the town centre. Dedham Hall (left), is the old grammar school where Constable studied; he walked here each day from his home at East Bergholt. Dedham is an ideal starting point for a stroll along the banks of the river to Flatford Mill, the scene of many of Constable's best-known paintings. Just beyond Flatford Mill is Willy Lott's cottage which is depicted in *The Hay Wain*, the most famous of all English landscape paintings. The church of St Mary the Virgin (right) was a favourite of Constable and the church often features in his work. It has one of Constable's few religious paintings, *The Ascension*, which hangs in the nave opposite the north porch.

FINCHINGFIELD

Situated between Saffron Walden and Braintree, this picture postcard settlement close to Constable Country has a quaint village green, duckpond, windmill and a number of medieval houses known as "cabbaches". It is easy to see why Finchingfield is often described as "the most photographed village in Essex"

Everything in Finchingfield is picture perfect, from the charming medieval and Georgian houses grouped around the village green to the duckpond and narrow bridge straddling the

stream. Several of the cottages have decorative pargetting on their walls – a feature typical of many old buildings in this part of Essex. The squat tower of the church of St John the Baptist stands at the top of Church Hill towering behind the Causeway Tea Cottage, housed in a charming 15th century dwelling. The church is well worth a visit and the streets around it are the ideal vantage point from which to look down on the village green.

FRAMLINGHAM

Situated 18 miles north-east of Ipswich, Framlingham has an attractive market square – the Market Hill – and is home to one of eastern England's most spectacular castles

The town sign stands in one corner of the triangular-shaped Market Hill and features the old water pump; sited on the corner of Albert Place and Fore Street, the pump was used to fill tall water-carts which supplied outlying houses and sprinkled water onto roads to settle down dust. Framlingham Castle is a magnificent landmark with 13 towers linked by a curtain wall. Dramatic views of the reed-fringed mere and surrounding town and countryside can be enjoyed from the battlements. The castle has an intriguing and chequered history, and over the years has been used as a fortress, an Elizabethan prison, a school and a poor house. It was here in 1553 that Mary Tudor was proclaimed Queen. Local allotment-holders (right) enjoy spectacular views of the castle and Framlingham College.

GRANTCHESTER

Located on the west bank of the river Cam a few miles from Cambridge, Grantchester is best-known for its picturesque riverside meadows, the popular Orchard Tea Garden and for its associations with the poet Rupert Brooke

The trip from Cambridge to Grantchester through the meadows is a memorable experience whether on foot or by punt. Close to the landing stage, it is a short stroll to one of Grantchester's most popular attractions, the Orchard Tea Rooms next door to the Old Vicarage. This spot proved to be so captivating that the poet Rupert Brooke moved to Orchard House in 1909, before later moving into The Old Vicarage next door. Brooke immortalised afternoon tea in the Orchard close to the church of St Andrew & St Mary when he wrote his poem *The Old Vicarage, Grantchester*, with its famous lines:

> *Stands the church clock at ten*
> * to three*
> *And is there honey still for tea?*

Brooke died at the early age of 27 of blood poisoning on the way to the First World War battlefield of Gallipoli. His statue now stands in front of the Old Vicarage.

GREAT MASSINGHAM

A picture postcard village east of King's Lynn, Great Massingham has an enormous village green and several attractive large ponds, some of which were used as fishponds for the 11th century Augustinian abbey which once stood here. Little Massingham lies a few miles to the north

The great square tower of St Mary's church dominates the village skyline and houses four bells. The church has a magnificent 13th century porch. Once a year the church is used to display artefacts associated with the now disused Massingham airfield to the east of the village, a centre of bomber command during the Second World War.

The village sign (above) represents Great Massingham's agricultural heritage and its former 11th century Augustinian abbey. The Peddars Way long-distance trail links this area with the coastal villages of north Norfolk. It passes to the west of the village and crosses Massingham Heath with its old flintmines and burial mounds.

HEACHAM

A popular holiday resort situated between King's Lynn and Hunstanton, Heacham is blessed with two wonderful unspoilt beaches. It is much loved by visitors for its panoramic views across the Wash and its dramatic sunsets

Heacham faces west and so visitors enjoy uninterrupted views across the 20-mile flat landscape of the Wash towards a horizon which seems entirely made up of sky – hence the reputation of the area for vivid sunsets. The village and beaches retain an unspoilt atmosphere attracting visitors who enjoy old-fashioned family holidays. Heacham is home to England's premier lavender farm (left), based at Caley Mill, where over 150 varieties of lavender are cultivated. The farm hosts an annual Lavender Festival each July when the crop is harvested and distilled. Just north of Heacham is the resort of Hunstanton with its eye-catching striped cliffs, a popular spot for fossil-hunters.

HICKLING

Hickling Broad is the largest of the navigable lakes in the Broads. The moorings at Hickling Broad, close to the Pleasure Boat Inn with their picturesque thatched boathouses, are a popular port of call for pleasurecraft

Fed by the river Thurne, Hickling Broad covers more than 346 acres and is surrounded by the largest reedbed in England. The Broad is maintained as a nature reserve by the Norfolk Wildlife Trust. The scattered village spreads north from the staithe at Hickling Heath with groups of houses interspersed amongst marsh and farmland. The village sign incorporates the ruined priory founded in 1185 as well as four roundels depicting a reed-cutter, swallow-tailed butterfly, the bittern and a peat-digger.

The large church of St Mary contains an unusual surprise: a tomb at the east end of the north aisle is covered with mysterious 17th century graffiti including a number of hands, drawn around, initialled and dated. There are also templates for Nine Men's Morris, a board game of the time.

HOLME NEXT THE SEA

Located between Hunstanton and Burnham Market in an area of outstanding natural beauty, Holme stands at the seaward end of the Peddars Way – a long-distance footpath which starts at Knettishall in Suffolk. This is an area of spectacular beaches backed by rolling sand dunes

The broad-towered church of St Mary (right) was almost completely rebuilt in 1779; the previous church was too large for the congregation and had fallen into disrepair, and a decision was taken to demolish the nave and the north and south aisles and build a smaller church. It has a simple yet attractive interior with some interesting stonework, including three separate fonts.

The main attraction of Holme is its seemingly endless beach and the mass of sand dunes which stretch from the shores of the Wash in the west to the far side of Brancaster Bay in the east. This is a key migration point for wild birds. The Norfolk Naturalist Trust runs the Holme Bird Observatory Trust and has a number of birdwatching hides. An ancient tree ring (dubbed "sea henge") which is now in the museum at Flag End near Peterborough was discovered on the sands at Holme beach.

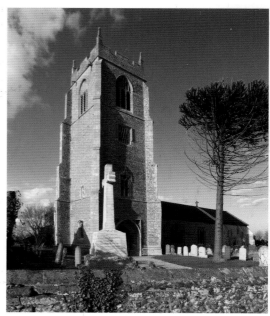

HORSEY

A tiny rural village north-west of Great Yarmouth and a mile from the coast, Horsey is situated in an area of outstanding natural beauty. Horsey Mill, the restored windpump which stands proudly beside the edge of Horsey Mere, is a well-known landmark in this area of the Broads

Horsey has an enviable location close to Braydon Marshes and the 129 acres of Horsey Mere. Less than a mile from the sea, Horsey is the closest Broadland village to the coast. The Horsey Estate was acquired by the National Trust from the Buxton family in 1948 and Horsey Mill, a beautifully restored five-storey redbrick drainage windpump, provides striking views across the Norfolk Broads from its top storey. The estate is internationally important for wildlife and is a prime location for birdwatching.

The church of All Saints (below) stands on a wooded knoll, the only high spot in a region of flat fields and drainage ditches. The church has a reed-thatched roof and a tall elegant octagonal bell tower, typical of many of the "rounded" church towers of north Norfolk. The exquisite stained-glass window at All Saints church is a commemorative portrait of Catherine Ursula Rising who died in 1890. She was the wife of Charles Rising who owned the Horsey Estate. Catherine is holding an artist's palette and is standing in a room at Horsey Hall

KIMBOLTON

Seven miles north-west of St Neots, historic Kimbolton is set amongst undulating fields close to Grafham Water. Its attractive wide high street, formerly the market square, is lined with brightly painted Georgian town houses and visitors can take a fascinating Town Walk to explore the heart of this picturesque small town

The centrepiece of Kimbolton is the castle (below) which forms the main building of Kimbolton School. The original castle was the home of Catherine of Aragon, Henry VIII's first wife who was banished to the castle following her divorce and who died here in 1536. The castle gatehouse, which stands at one end of the glorious High Street, was designed by Robert Adam and built between 1764-6. The High Street is the centre of a conservation area which extends outwards to encompass over 80 listed buildings. Since the 13th century Kimbolton has held an annual fair – the Statute Fair, or the "Statty" as it is known locally. It is held every September and the High Street is closed to traffic.

LITTLE WALSINGHAM

The sister hamlets of Great and Little Walsingham lie in the vale of the river Stiffkey, between Wells-next-the-Sea and Fakenham. Little Walsingham, the larger of the two villages, is famous for its Anglican and Roman Catholic shrines which attract thousands of pilgrims each year

In 1061, Lady Richeldis, widow of the local lord of the manor, saw an apparition of the Virgin Mary. Mary instructed Lady Richeldis to build a replica of the house in Nazareth where the angel Gabriel gave Mary news of the birth of Jesus. The shrine of Our Lady of Walsingham quickly became a medieval place of pilgrimage until it was destroyed on the orders of Henry VIII. In the early 20th century the shrine was restored and now thousands of pilgrims each year follow the procession from the church of St Mary (below) to the Abbey Grounds. They traditionally walk the mile and a half to the Slipper Chapel, centre of the Roman Catholic shrine, where pilgrims leave their shoes before walking on to the Holy House, centre of the Church of England shrine.

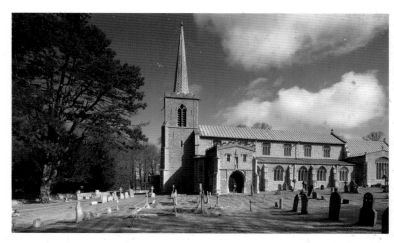

Little Walsingham's attractive timber-framed houses, many with red pantiled roofs, can be seen along the High Street which broadens out into a square, called Common Place. In the middle of the square is a 16th century octagonal pumphouse with a weathered door (middle left). The iron brazier mounted on top of the pumphouse was once the only permanent light in the village.

LAVENHAM

Situated north-east of Sudbury in Suffolk, Lavenham has often been described as "England's finest medieval town". Its many narrow winding streets are lined with beautifully preserved half-timbered houses and small painted cottages

One of Lavenham's jewels is the 141ft high tower of St Peter and St Paul's church (below right), constructed from knapped flint, which sits proudly at the top of the hill in an immaculately manicured churchyard. The church interior contains some fascinating and amusing 15th century carvings, including one of a man squeezing a pig to make it squeal. Artists and photographers are drawn to the many half-timbered medieval cottages and, in the marketplace, the 16th century Guildhall and the market cross, where bear-baiting once took place, are a great attraction. Other buildings of note are the Old Wool Hall, now part of the Swan Inn, the Little Hall, a late 14th century medieval hall house and the building now housing the Crooked House Art Gallery (right) built in 1425.

MALDON

Situated at the head of the Blackwater estuary, Maldon is home to many of the historic and colourful Thames sailing barges which plied between this part of Essex and the capital during the 18th and 19th centuries. Maldon was the scene of a famous encounter during the Viking invasion when local defenders were defeated in an epic battle fought out on the mudflats in front of the town

Thames sailing barges were once the maritime workhorses of eastern England and many of these historic craft can be seen moored up by the Jolly Sailor Inn at Hythe Quay. They once carried cargo including hay from the farmlands of Essex to London as feed and bedding for horses – hence their nickname "haystackers" due to the piles of hay on deck. The boats were built with flat bottoms so that they could easily navigate the shallow estuaries and rest up in the muddy creeks and inlets of the Essex coast at low tide. All Saints church has a unique triangular tower often used as a reference point for sailors in the estuary. Hythe Quay and the adjoining Promenade Park are ideal spots to view the estuary and there is a walk out to the promontory where a statue depicts Brythnoth, earl of Essex, who died fighting the Vikings at the Battle of Maldon in 991. The statue faces towards Northey Island where the skirmish took place.

MUCH HADHAM

A few miles west of Bishop's Stortford, Much Hadham is one of Hertfordshire's oldest and prettiest villages. Set in the Ash valley and surrounded by open woodland, the village's main glory is the High Street, a mixture of Elizabethan cottages and fine 18th and 19th century residences

Much Hadham can justifiably claim to have been instrumental in creating the Tudor dynasty as it was the birthplace of Edmund Tudor, father of the first Tudor king, Henry VII. The nearby village of Perry Green was home to the famous sculptor Henry Moore who is now buried at St Thomas's church. One of Moore's works, *Heads of a King and Queen*, completed in 1953, is in the large parish churchyard of St Andrew's. On the outskirts of the village, at Sheepfield Barn, Perry Green, is a sculpture park dedicated to Henry Moore where many of his statues can be seen and which has exhibitions featuring modern art and sculpture.

An interesting building just north of the church, "The Palace" or Manor House, has had a chequered history and still contains timbers from a 14th century hall. The Manor House has been used as an asylum and a school; it is now privately owned. The Forge Museum in the high street contains a working forge and has a beautiful Victorian garden.

NORTHILL AND ICKWELL

Three miles west of Biggleswade, the village of Ickwell Green lies just south of its close neighbour Northill in an area of market gardens. Together with the tiny hamlets of Lower Caldicote, Hatch and Thorncote these two villages make up the small parish of Northill centred around the valley of the river Ivel

The picturesque village green at Ickwell is flanked by brightly coloured cottages. On the edge of the green stands the yellow-washed pavilion of the Ickwell Green cricket club, one of the oldest sporting clubs in Bedfordshire. The green has a maypole, centre of the annual Mayday festival which dates back to the 16th century. The 14th century church of St Mary in the centre of the village of Northill is known for its 17th century painted glass and the one-handed clock mounted on its spire built by master clockmaker Thomas Tompion. He was born in Ickwell at the former smithy close to the village green.

PAVENHAM

Six miles north-west of Bedford, the peaceful and unspoilt village of Pavenham is surrounded by gentle rolling hills and rich arable farmland

The Great Ouse meanders its way lazily through a wooded valley just south of the village and there are attractive footpaths in both directions along its northern bank at the southern end of Mill Lane which runs down from the High Street. These paths form part of a circular walk around the village taking in local farms and skirting the edge of Pavenham Park golf club. The common bullrush which grows profusely along the Great Ouse was the source of Pavenham's famous rushwork industry which dates back to the Middle Ages. The rushes were harvested using long rounded "billhooks" mounted on the ends of long poles. Harvesters would wade into the river and use their poles to cut the reeds free. The reeds were then dried and made into rolls of rush matting. Pavenham matting was used to cover floors in the Palace of Westminster well into the 20th century.

ORFORD

Orford was once a coastal port but the shingle spit of Orford Ness which stretches down the coast from Aldeburgh has gradually enclosed the village and it now stands on the west bank of the river Alde

Orford grew up around a 12th century royal castle; the remains of its restored keep (right) dominate the town and the surrounding flat countryside. The village comes to life in the summer when pleasure-craft and sailing boats tie up along the breezy quay. The estuaries of the river Alde and Ore provide a long stretch of sheltered water, perfect for sailing thanks to the protection of Orford Ness. The prominent church of St Bartholomew, parts of which date from 1166, boasts a remarkable font. Close by are the remains of the castle built by Henry II to defend the area against seaborne invasion. Today, visitors come to the area to visit the keep and enjoy spectacular views from the top of the battlements or to explore Havergate Bird Sanctuary and walk the large shingle spit of Orford Ness. The spit is the site of the Orford Ness national nature reserve; owned by the National Trust it includes a working lighthouse which sits at the end of the 13 mile spit. There is also a redundant atomic research station, whose pagoda-shaped buildings are clearly visible from the Quay at Orford.

RENDHAM

A quiet traditional Suffolk village on the river Alde, three miles west of Saxmundham. The attractive village sign incorporates the local church of St Michael and the famous Roman head associated with the village

In 1907, Arthur Godbold, a pupil at Rendham School, uncovered a bronze head, part of a life-size statue of the Roman emperor Claudius, whilst swimming in the river Alde. Theories differ as to how such an important piece of sculpture found its way here, but one explanation is that the statue was pulled down from the Roman camp at Colchester during the sacking of the town by British tribal leader Boudicca in AD60. A permanent display illustrating the discovery and history of the head is on show in the church of St Michael at the centre of village. The church also boasts some exquisite stained-glass panels and a set of the royal arms of King Charles II on the south nave wall dating from the 1660s. The White Horse Inn (above), just opposite the church, is at the heart of village life and has won many accolades for its traditional beer and food.

RUMBURGH

Sited on East Anglian claylands, the village of Rumburgh, surrounded by irregular small fields with pollarded hedgerow oaks, is a peaceful rural village in an ancient medieval landscape

The High Suffolk and South Norfolk claylands is a plateau area of predominantly flat chalky boulder cay punctuated by several small streams, rivers and the river Waveney, with a long tradition of farming. Mentioned in the Norfolk entries of the Domesday Book, Rumburgh was originally part of the neighbouring village of Wissett. A Benedictine Priory was founded here by Aethelmar, Bishop of Norwich, in 1064 but all that remains now is the village church. The village is an ideal location for cycling, walking and birdwatching with the Heritage Coast close by, including Southwold, Aldeburgh and the RSPB reserve at Minsmere.

There is a traditional May Day fete each year when local people gather together to celebrate the spring festival. At the centre of the village is the attractive Rumburgh Buck Inn, parts of which date from the 15th century. North-east of the village lies the Norfolk and Suffolk Aviation Museum at Flixton which houses a large collection of aircraft dating from the Second World War.

SALTHOUSE

Between Cley next the Sea and Sheringham on the north Norfolk coast, Salthouse was once a place where salt, produced from seawater at Sarbury Hill to the west of the village, was stored. This is an area where the sea periodically breaks through the fragile coastal pebble banks and inundates the surrounding countryside, leaving lagoons of brackish water which attract a wide variety of wading birds

In the past Salthouse villagers relied heavily on the local environment for their survival, when both heath and marsh were a vital source of food and heating. Managing and cutting gorse to feed the bakehouse and cutting "flags" (peat) for household fires is still remembered by some of the older inhabitants. The village itself is a small settlement of flint and whitewashed cottages with a post office and a local pub, the Dun Cow. To the back of the village the land rises quite steeply and from the top of the ridge at Salthouse Heath there are extensive views of the village. Its handsome church, with its beautiful stained-glass windows (left), is dedicated to St Nicholas, the patron saint of fishermen.

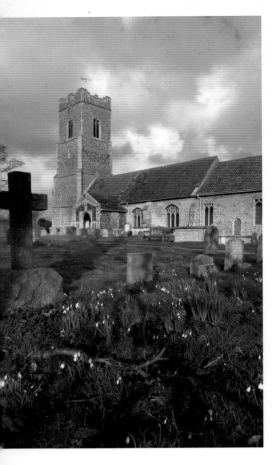

SNAPE

Snape Maltings is a unique cluster of restored 19th century malthouses and granaries nestling on the banks of the river Alde, five miles inland from Aldeburgh. The site includes galleries, shops, restaurants and a world-class concert hall. The Maltings is the centre of the Aldeburgh international music festival which was founded by the composer Benjamin Britten in 1948

Most of the Maltings buildings date from around 1850, when local businessman Newson Garrett discovered that this was an ideal location to malt local barley and ship it to London breweries. The nearby quay was built to accommodate barges bringing coal to the maltings and carrying malt to breweries. In 1965 malting became uneconomic and the first concert hall was built. It was tragically destroyed by fire in 1969, but was rebuilt in time for the following year's music festival; the adjacent barley store was converted into the Britten-Pears School in 1979.

The church of St John the Baptist (above) stands on high ground approximately one mile north of the village and a short walk from the Maltings. The nave was built in the 13th century and the tower and porch added in the 15th century.

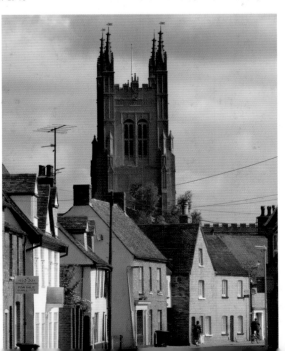

ST NEOTS

The largest town in Cambridgeshire, St Neots is situated on the Great Ouse which meanders peacefully through the town and forms the border with the historic county of Huntingdonshire. At its heart is Market Square, laid out in the 12th century and still very much in use today

St Neots developed because of its geographical position: first as the site of a ford across the Great Ouse and then as a stopping-off place on the main road to London; later it became a station on the main London to Edinburgh railway line. St Neots was the site of a medieval priory built to house the remains of the Cornish monk Neot, who had been canonised for his work in helping the poor. His bones were brought to the settlement in order to attract pilgrims and a market developed. The growing town was granted a market charter in 1130 and continued to flourish but the priory did not survive the Dissolution. The town has several attractive riverside walks and competitive rowing is believed to have commenced here in 1865 with the first full rowing regatta held in 1874. Today the tower of the church of St Mary (left), known as the "cathedral of Huntingdonshire", dominates the town.

SOUTHWOLD

An elegant seaside town, Southwold stands at the northern end of the Suffolk Heritage Coast and has an atmosphere and charm that is quintessentially English. Bounded by the North Sea to the east, the river Blyth and Southwold harbour to the south-west and Buss Creek to the north, the town is almost an island in the midst of reedy marshland

Over 300 beautifully painted beach huts (above) line the shore at Southwold; they evolved from the many Victorian fishermen's and bathers' huts on the shoreline. The huts are lifted each autumn from the beach by a giant crane to keep them safe from the high winter tides and strong gales. In 1973, exceptionally high tides caused severe flooding in the area when the water level reached over the top of the door of the Harbour Inn, next to the sailing club. The river Blyth flows into the North Sea a short distance south of the town and at high tide a sheltered inland estuary, ideal for sailing enthusiasts, is formed stretching as far inland as Blythburgh.

Southwold lighthouse (built between 1886 and 1889) stands, unusually, in the middle of the town (below). It was built here to protect the building from the encroaching sea and because it was better able to mark the dangerous sands to the north of the town.

SUTTON BRIDGE

Sutton Bridge lies at the junction of three counties – Lincolnshire, Norfolk and Cambridgeshire. Situated three miles from the Wash on the river Nene, the village owes its development to the building of a bridge at this strategic point

Two hundred years ago the Lincolnshire village of Sutton Bridge was a small hamlet consisting of a few farmhouses and cottages scattered along a narrow track. Crossing this low-lying area which drains northwards into the Wash was treacherous, with wagons and coaches often getting lost in the quicksand and marshes of Cross Keys Marsh which lay to the east and north. Even at low water, finding a safe passage across the saltmarsh was difficult and travellers would often stop at the Wash House (now the Bridge Hotel) and hire a guide to help them make their way through the ever-changing terrain. The first bridge across the Nene was designed by Rennie & Telford and opened in 1831; it stimulated the growth of the village and a sizeable port developed with wharves and warehouses. The current swing bridge – the Crosskeys Bridge – opened in 1897 and is the third bridge to cross the river. Today Sutton Bridge is a fast-growing village and the centre of much agricultural work.

Swaffham Prior

The picturesque village of Swaffham Prior, situated between Cambridge and Newmarket, is unusual in that it has twin churches, St Mary's and St Cyriac's, standing side-by-side in the same churchyard. Swaffham Prior's splendid restored windmill – Foster's Windmill – stands on Mill Hill

The church of St Mary and the church of St Cyriac & St Julitta (right) both sit on top of a grass slope rising steeply away from the main street. In the middle ages, almost all citizens were tied to the lord of the local manor who built a church for his vassals. By chance, in Swaffham Prior, two lords with adjoining manors chose locations on the

outer edges of their land which placed two churches in close proximity. In 1667, the two parishes were amalgamated and the parishioners adopted St Mary as their place of worship. The unusual stained-glass windows in St Mary's (left) commemorate those who served in the First World War. The church of St Cyriac's gradually fell into disrepair. It has now been restored and serves as a hall for meetings and exhibitions. The Scottish poet and author Edwin Muir made his home at Swaffham Prior and is buried in the churchyard. Foster's Windmill, depicted on the village sign, was built by local millwrights Frysons of Soham in 1857. The Foster family owned and worked the mill until it closed in 1946. The mill was rescued in 1970 and later restored; in 1992 it began to grind corn again. It is one of only two working tower mills in Cambridgeshire.

Thaxted

With its superb architecture and magnificent church, the small town of Thaxted has something for everyone – from its splendid old windmill to Morris dancing and a summer music festival

Situated near the river Chelmer south of Saffron Walden, Thaxted is considered by many to be the jewel in the crown of Essex. The town is dominated by the steeple of the cathedral-like church of St John, and is full of harmonious groups of buildings to charm the visitor. Behind the church John Webb's mill of 1804 is framed by the almshouses. Winding streets full of half-timbered and beautifully painted houses seem to lead towards the church which was presided over for many years by the Rev Conrad Noel, who did much to galvanise the spiritual and musical energies of the town. His wife, Miriam Noel, was responsible in 1911 for the revival of the traditional pursuit of Morris dancing and today the annual gathering of Morris Men from all over England takes place in Thaxted on the first weekend after the spring bank holiday. The composer Gustav Holst fell in love with Thaxted while on a walking tour in 1913. He composed *The Planet Suite* while living in the town and there is a blue plaque to him on the house in which he lived from 1917-25. The annual Thaxted festival takes place in June and July. The double row of almshouses (right) situated in the churchyard was built as a priest's house, known as the Chantry.

TOLLESBURY

Situated among the saltmarsh and creeks of the Blackwater estuary, Tollesbury is known as the village of "the plough and the sail" because it made its living from both the land and the sea

In the Middle Ages Tollesbury was one of the richest parishes in the east of Essex. The village today retains its medieval pattern, with its streets radiating out from the marketplace, known as the Square. The beautiful church of St Mary the Virgin is situated on its southern edge at the highest point in the village. Tollesbury is surrounded by farms, marshland and creeks; records show that in the 19th century it was home to many seafarers and the Kings Head on the Square became known as the "seafarer's pub". Until the early 20th century barges were used to transport grain and fish to London because the road conditions were bad. The elegant wooden sail lofts (above) date from the Edwardian era and were built to serve the needs of both the local fishing fleet and the sailing fraternity. Tollesbury Marina (below) is a family boating centre and has a swimming pool, tennis courts and yacht chandlery. Other attractions include the beautiful Tollesbury Granary which featured in the BBC series *Restoration Village*.

WALPOLE ST PETER

The magnificent church at Walpole St Peter is one of the finest in England. Known as "the Cathedral of the Fenlands", it is hidden away in the countryside between Holbeach and King's Lynn, just south of the A17 into north Norfolk

Once Walpole St Peter and Walpole St Andrew were two separate villages but they are now linked into one settlement. The famous 13th century church hosts a spectacular annual flower festival and welcomes visitors from all over the country. The great landowning family the Walpoles hailed from the villages of Walpole St Peter and Walpole Cross Keys (a few miles to the north); Sir Robert Walpole (1676-1745), whose life's work was the creation of the great mansion at Houghton Hall, became Britain's first Prime Minister. Walpole Water Gardens is a superb visitor attraction with exotic plants, 20 different kinds of eucalyptus, palms, bananas and grasses, black swans, ornamental ducks and koi carp.

WALBERSWICK

From the 13th century to the First World War Walberswick was a thriving port, trading in bacon, cheese, timber and fish. Its superb beach and panoramic vistas have long attracted artists, including Charles Rennie Mackintosh and the English Impressionist Philip Wilson Steer who immortalised the beach and the pier in his paintings

Linked to the neighbouring town of Southwold by a ferry across the river Blyth, Walberswick is a popular resort with its attractive harbour and village green surrounded by quaint houses. The area around Walberswick is a protected area of outstanding natural beauty, and is made up chiefly of marshland and heath. St Andrew's church (right) at the top of the village is an impressive building and clearly shows how prosperous the settlement must have been around the 15th century. In 1492, a new church was built to replace the old one.

WEST NEWTON

*The attractive village of West Newton is part
of the Sandringham estate, which also
includes the villages of Wolferton, Appleton,
Flitcham, Anmer and Sherbourne*

The Sandringham estate (left) is situated in an area of outstanding natural beauty close to the north Norfolk coast. The pretty estate village of West Newton boasts a cluster of flint and rubble buildings including the primary school (right), located in the centre of the village close to the church. The unusual bench (below) provides a strong focal point for a village panorama. In 2006 the Prince of Wales and the Duchess of Cornwall attended the Sandringham Flower Show when the event celebrated its 125th anniversary; later in the year the Prince of Wales opened a farm shop in the village which specialises in local produce and cuts of meat from rare breeds of farm animal.

WESTMILL

*The pretty village of Westmill is one mile south of Buntingford in the
peaceful backwater of the Rib valley. The village green is overlooked by
the Anglo-Saxon church of St Mary the Virgin with its
distinctive square tower*

The village of Westmill nestles in the north-east corner of Hertfordshire. It owes its name to the three mills that stood beside the river Rib when the Domesday Book was compiled. The manor of West Mill was granted by William the Conqueror to Robert de Olgi. The village green, with its attractive period houses, is overlooked by the Norman parish church (above) of St Mary the Virgin which dates from this period. The triangular-shaped village green has a distinctive covered water pump at its centre. On the edge of the green are the cottages known as Pilgrim's Row built by Samuel Pilgrim in the early 1700s. There is also a fine turreted village hall and The Westmill Tea Room.

WOODBRIDGE

Situated on the river Deben, not far from the coast, Woodbridge is famous for its superb Tide Mill – one of only four in the country. Sutton Hoo, just across the river, is the burial place of Saxon kings. The story of this remarkable discovery is chronicled in the Woodbridge Museum

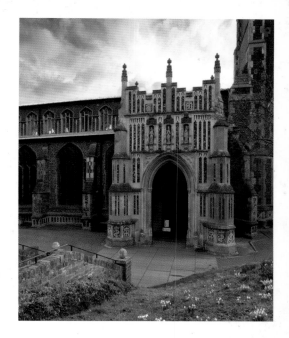

During the early 7th century East Anglia flourished under its ruler, Redwald of Rendlesham. When he died he was interred at Sutton Hoo, one of Britain's most important and atmospheric archaeological sites, the burial ground of the Anglo-Saxon kings of East Anglia. The site is now owned by the National Trust and there is a superb visitor centre and exhibiton hall.

The pretty town of Woodbridge bristles with independent shops, restaurants and cafes. The beautiful Tide Mill (bottom) was a working mill until 1957 when its oak shaft broke. In 1982 it was fully restored and opened to the public. The splendid Shire Hall (below) stands in the centre of the

town, in the middle of Market Hill. It was built in 1575 by Thomas Seckford, Master of the Court of Requests to Queen Elizabeth I. The grand church of St Mary's (right), with its magnificent north porch, is one of England's greatest churches. Rebuilt in the 15th century, the best view of its fine tower can be had from the quayside. Woodbridge is famous for the variety of elegant doors which grace many of its splendid buildings. Cumberland Street, in the centre of the town, has some fine examples.

First published in 2009 by Myriad Books Limited
35 Bishopsthorpe Road,
London SE26 4PA

Photographs copyright © John Potter
Text copyright © John Potter

John Potter has asserted his right under the
Copyright, Designs and Patents Act 1998 to be
identified as the author of this work.

ISBN 1 84746 254 5
EAN 978 1 84746 254 1

Designed by Jerry Goldie Graphic Design
Map Stephen Dew

Printed in China

www.myriadbooks.com

Front cover: Great Massingham; back cover: Little
Walsingham (top) and Thaxted (below): title
page: Willie Lott's cottage, Dedham Vale (top);
pargetting detail on a house at Ashwell
(below)

A selection of John Potter's work can be seen
at his website:

www.jpotter-landscape-photographer.com